I Can Count

Counting in the Sea

Rebecca Rissman

www.raintreepublishers.co.uk
Visit our website to find out
more information about
Raintree books.

To order:
☎ Phone 0845 6044371
🖹 Fax +44 (0) 1865 312263
🖱 Email myorders@raintreepublishers.co.uk

Customers from outside the UK please telephone +44 1865 312262

Raintree is an imprint of Capstone Global Library Limited, a
company incorporated in England and Wales having its registered
office at 7 Pilgrim Street, London, EC4V 6LB – Registered company
number: 6695582

Edited by Rebecca Rissman, Dan Nunn, and Catherine Veitch
Designed by Steve Mead
Picture research by Mica Brancic
Originated by Capstone Global Library Ltd
Production by Alison Parsons
Printed in China

ISBN 978 1 406 24099 3 (hardback)
16 15 14 13 12
10 9 8 7 6 5 4 3 2 1

ISBN 978 1 406 24104 4 (paperback)
17 16 15 14 13
10 9 8 7 6 5 4 3 2 1

British Library Cataloguing in Publication Data
Rissman, Rebecca.
Counting in the sea. – (I can count!)
513.2'11-dc23
A full catalogue record for this book is available from the
British Library.

Acknowledgements
We would like to thank the following for permission to reproduce
photographs: Shutterstock p. 5 (© borisha), pp. 6-7 (© Eric Isselée),
pp. 8-9 (© Catmando), p. 10 (© JCElv), p. 11 (© gracious_tiger, ©
WitthayaP), pp. 12-13 (© Madlen), pp. 14-15 (© Eric Isselée), pp.
16-17 (© Rich Carey), pp. 18-19 (© Teguh Tirtaputra), pp. 20-21 (©
Johannes Kornelius), pp. 22-23 (© Irina Kovancova).

Front cover photograph of three garibaldi fish reproduced with
permission of Shutterstock (© Joe Belanger).
Back cover photographs of a crab reproduced with permission
of Shutterstock (© Eric Isselée), and a sea star reproduced with
permission of Shutterstock (© Madlen).

Every effort has been made to contact copyright holders of any
material reproduced in this book. Any omissions will be rectified in
subsequent printings if notice is given to the publisher.

Contents

3

5

4

10

7

8

1

2

6

9

Can you count **one** seagull,
flying near the shore?

5

Can you count **two** funny crabs, on the ocean floor?

7

Can you count **three** giant whales, gliding through the deep?

6 7 8 9 10

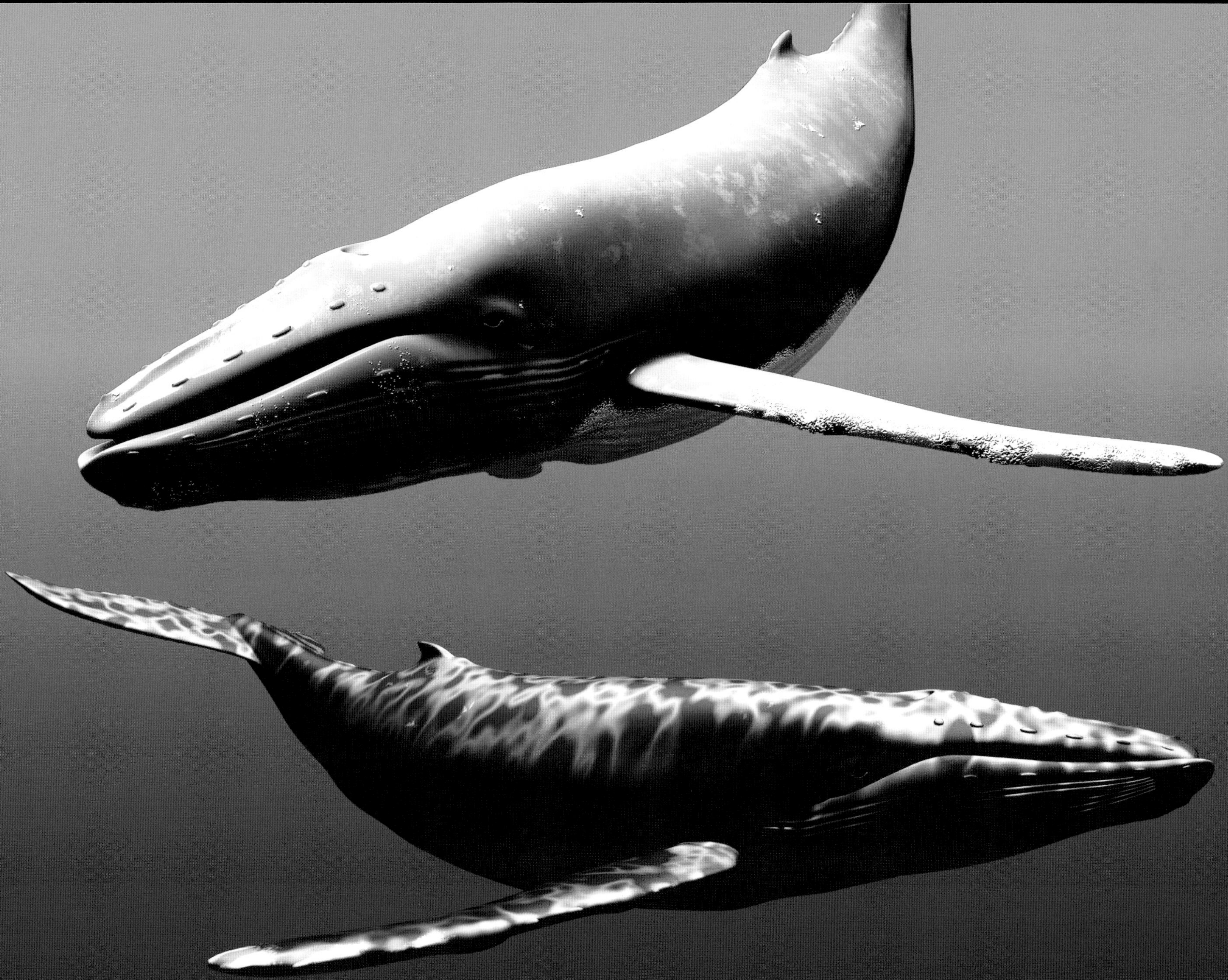

Can you count **four** dolphins,
calling in clicks and beeps?

Can you count **five** starfish, clinging to this dock?

6 7 8 9 10

13

1 2 3 4 5

Can you count **six** tiny shrimp,
underneath this rock?

14

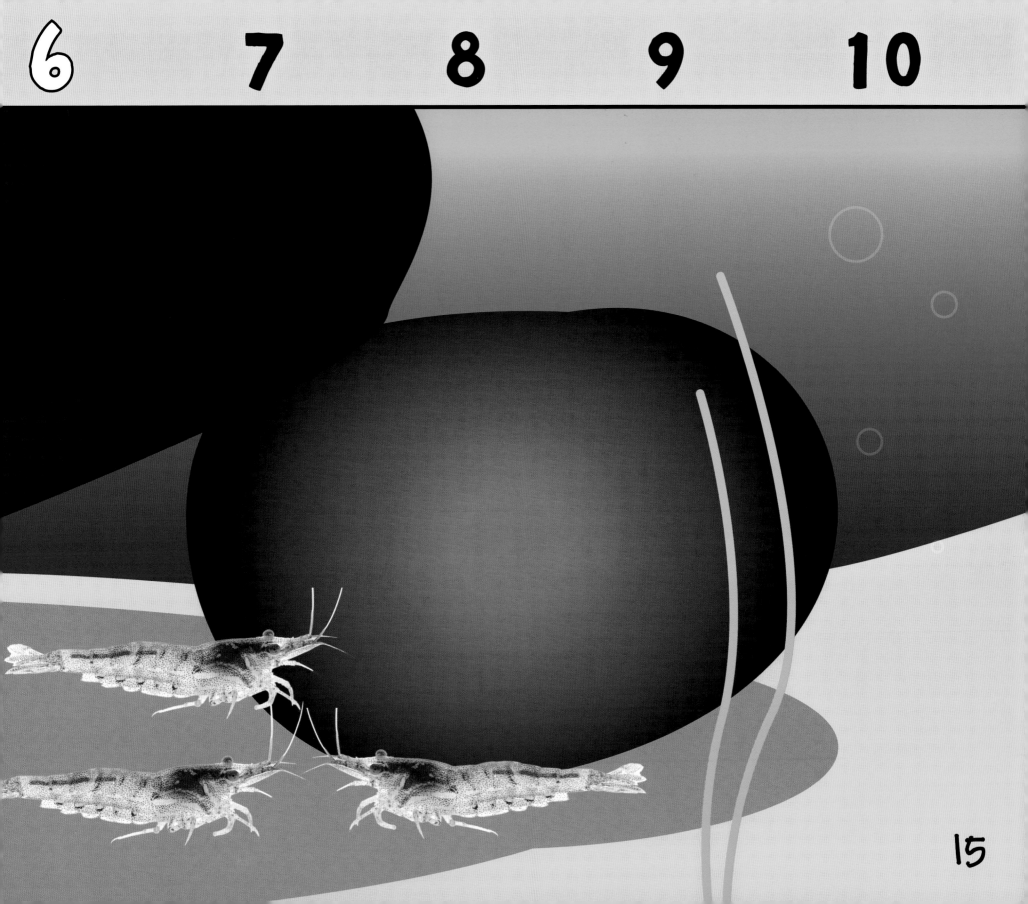

15

Can you count **Seven** turtles?
They can't travel very fast!

Can you count **eight** octopuses?
One has shot an inky blast!

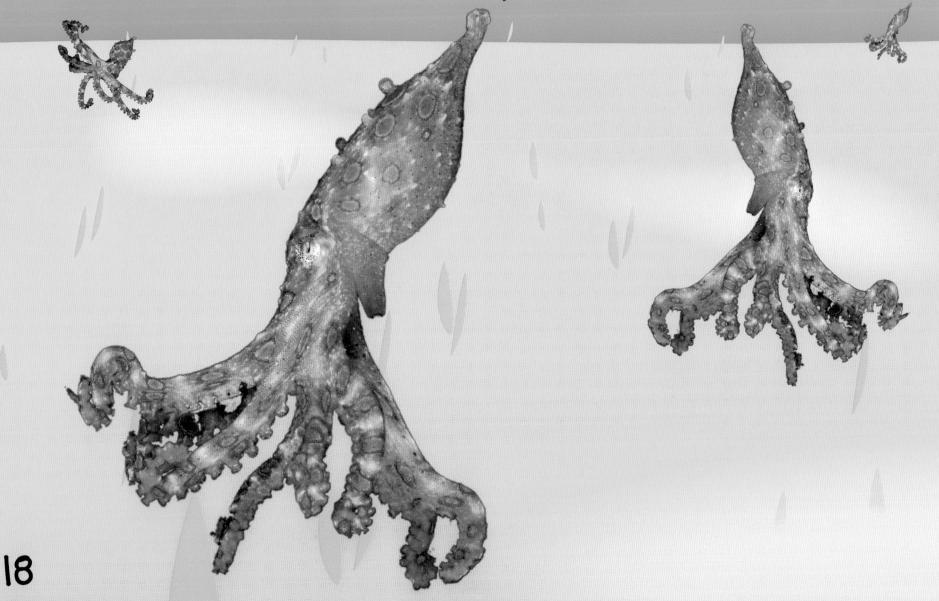

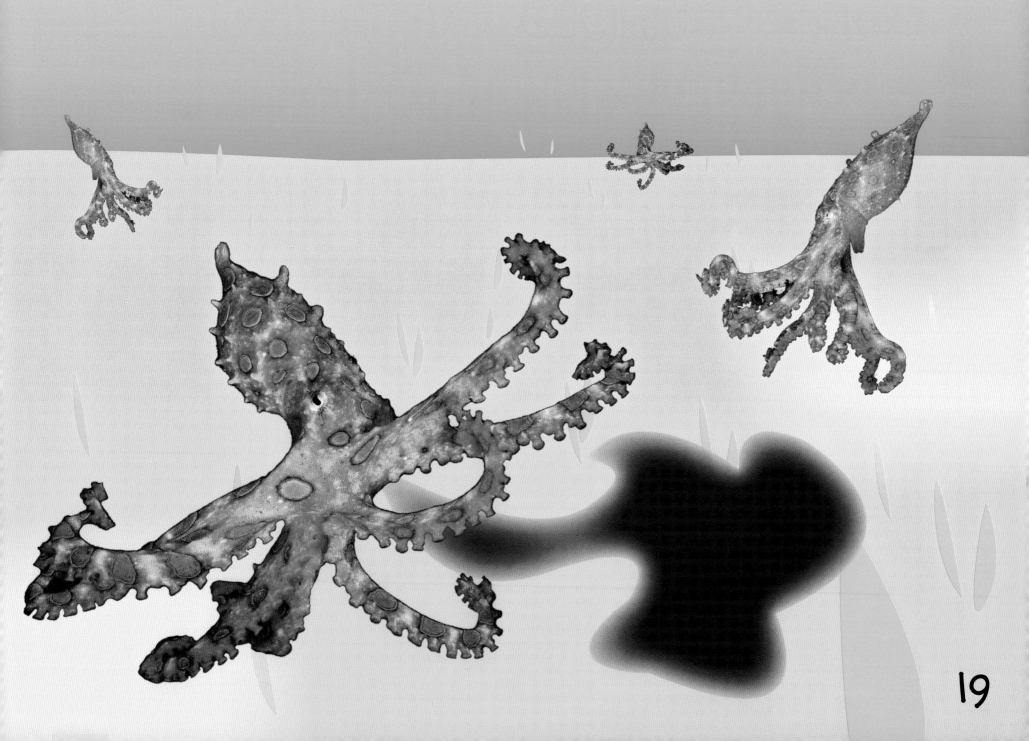

Can you count **nine** little fish, in orange, black, and white?

21

Can you count **ten** jellyfish?
They're quite a scary sight!

23

Guess the number
Which number comes next?

1, 2, 3, 4, ?   2, 3, 4, 5, ?

6, 7, 8, 9, ?   10, 9, 8, 7, ?

Index